To   Helen

It is
Beyond
Me

With love,
Nadera

———

First published in Great Britain in 2021 by
Healing 4 Humanity Publishing

Copyright © 2021 by Nadira Seeram
Formatting by The Amethyst Angel

ISBN: 978-1-7397579-0-8

The moral right of the author has been asserted.

First Edition

"Several years ago, when I was at a crossroads in my life, I called out for a guru to teach and enlighten. She appeared in the form of Nadira. This book is her amazing story that many of us have also experienced. She shows us an ability to rise up, to be broken open, to hold on to each other. In spite of the challenges, to begin a healing process that can result in our empowerment. It is also a health and social issue of great importance for the women in our world. That healing is necessary to our lives, to change what appears to be the norm for so many of us in crisis stemming from family dynamics and ancestral trauma, to a conscious experience of spiritual enlightenment. Above all, it is her gift of healing, joy and of love that she has so willingly shared."

Dilsa Capdeville is a US Virgin Islands Social Worker, Therapist and Social Changemaker for the rights and protection of women and children suffering domestic violence, abuse and neglect.

Contents

The Greenness of My Mind

Pashley Down Infant School, Eastbourne, England, 1967.

I am five years old, and wearing a bright emerald green school cardigan. Its wool keeps me warm and soothes and comforts me on the inside. Wearing my green school cardigan gives me the feeling of being safe and cared for, a tangible feeling of belonging. It gives me permission and encouragement to explore safely and freely, which is not available to me anywhere else. It means I am visible and acknowledged, seen as well as heard. I am connected, alive and joyous. I love my teacher, I believe she loves me, and I love being at school.

My earliest happy memories are connected to wearing my green school cardigan. The colour green gives me instant recall and access to those happy experiences of belonging and safety. My love of green has never left me, it is the colour associated with the spiritual or soul heart, and it is the colour of universal love. It makes me smile.

When the heart is at peace, the consciousness can go beyond the mind, and explore unfathomable depths in the knowledge of safety and support.

But when the sense of connection is disrupted, fractured and torn, as I came to experience later, the mind can halt in its tracks, spinning its wheels relentlessly, going nowhere and without a place to rest.

My other love was for numbers. I loved numbers from the time I could count, and my teacher recognised this love and aptitude. They had a natural rhythm and logic, nothing could be hidden from them, and everything could be shown and made clear. Numbers made sense to me, and it was as if the world made sense through them. I saw how it all added up, nothing missing, nothing left out, everything fitting together. Numbers held information about how things worked, and they expanded into subtle yet tangible patterns which I could sense. I intrinsically knew that everything was described this way and could be brought to light this way, they were codes of vibration.

Later, I could feel algebra even before I understood it, and would admire equations for the sheer beauty of truth they displayed. The patterns of vibration were unlimited and always moving, in a constant flow as if in a dance with each other, sometimes receding, sometimes advancing. I also knew that there was only one undivided power behind it all, one orchestrator, which was my comfort.

No idea could be separated from it, no idea could be separated from another, and so no idea of separation could be real. It was a blow in later school years when my love of interwoven patterns was ridiculed in art lessons for being too abstract, because to me they were the reality of connection.

Even from this early age I felt without doubt, that all of life was made up of formulas, formulas that were the codes to unlocking and revealing the patterns of life.

Not only that, but there was a master formula that encapsulated everything, all parts and all systems. It was this belief that formed what I wanted to be when I grew up. A mathematician who would discover the master formula of life. I could picture myself in a large open study with glass doors all around, at a large desk wearing a white coat and spectacles, with large blackboards in the background. I do not know how old I was, but I clearly remember hearing and receiving my father's first, and one of only two, statements of encouragement and affirmation. He told me of a famous, genius female Indian mathematician, Shakuntala Devi. Just the knowledge of her existence left a huge impression on me, and inspired me to believe that I too could grasp the hidden mysteries of life.

I knew that the master formula would explain the workings of the mind, emotions, and actions. It would be the explainer of all explanations, the answer to the big 'why?' of what is seen and unseen, of what is acted out and what is held back. When we know why things are the way they are, then we know how to change them when they don't work. I particularly wanted to understand and resolve conflict, because that is what I saw and felt all around me, and later on, inside me. I wanted the full picture and the power to change it.

Fifty-four years later, I still feel warm waves of happiness whenever I pass the Pashley Down school-children, wearing their green school cardigans. Over the years, my family has come to associate the colour green with my sense of happiness. I receive many cards and gifts from children and grandchildren that are painted, decorated, or adorned in green. To me, it is the colour of life, a statement of connection and therefore the opening to all possibilities. I am incredibly grateful for that early awareness of connection. Even though I lost the emotional connection to my teacher when I moved school, I kept my connection to numbers, symbols and shapes, and to the colour green.

But as a child, my heart was not always at peace. An earlier memory from the year before I could wear that green school cardigan stands out in stark contrast.

My brother was five years older and already attending the local boys' junior school, and my sister, who was just a year older, had started at the infant school. I was at home on my own for a year before I could also start school, and what went on at home stayed at home.

We lived in a detached house overlooking a recreational ground. It had an old air raid shelter under a mound in the garden, loosely filled with rubble and stinging nettles, not a safe place to hide or to play. The garden was like an invading jungle, with tall grass, untended and left to its own devices. The jungle may have been reminiscent of my mother's impressions of growing up in Guyana (known in British colonial times as British Guiana). She was raised in the shadows of the caste system mentality merged with western subjugation.

There was a perceived difference between Indians living off the land nearer to old plantations and the rainforest of the interior, and Indians making their livelihoods from businesses in the capital Georgetown, the latter to which her family belonged. She was too proud to garden, but the result was that we got little good out of it. She felt she had been brought down in status, which was one of the designed effects of plantation life in the colonies.

Our house was always cold, with only electric storage heaters downstairs, the kind you could sit on and be warned of getting piles. There was a well-decorated sitting room where guests and visitors were entertained, and the upstairs bedrooms with their cold bare stone walls, where we could not and would not have wanted to take our friends, out of embarrassment. There was a back door in the kitchen which led to a tall back gate, an additional entrance and exit to the house.

My father would often come home from work at lunchtime. And just as often, he would go to the local bookmakers to place bets on the horse races. He had something of a reputation at the bookies. My mother did not shield her resentment of the way my father handled money, whether it was what he chose to gamble on or to invest in. She herself was very protective of her father's money that had been sequestered out of Guyana when foreign exchange became restricted. Money may have been part of the trigger on this occasion that I remember vividly. Whatever the spark was this time, they were continually triggering each other's insecurities, their narratives passed down and played out through conditions and controls of idealised love, place, and worth. Just like sibling fights and rivalries, they were in fact too alike, as they were biological first cousins. Trust and co-operation were not evident.

One day, while my siblings were at school, I remember my mother dragging me outside through the back door in the kitchen as she heard my father leaving by the back gate. She was pushing me at him, demanding that he take me with him. Of course, he did not want to take me, and neither did I want to go. I hardly ever wanted to be near him. I was caught in the middle of the screaming and shouting, pushing and pulling. This is my first vivid memory of seeing my father hit my mother, and not just once.

Terrified, what made it worse was that my reluctance to go with him became the cause of the problem. I was blamed by both for what I had done. I was guilty of being afraid and for not complying. This pattern was repeated many times over the years, and I carried on learning that my feelings did not count, I was irrelevant to the story. When in fact I was just re-enacting the same story of isolation and devaluation.

Confined and Controlled

In the mid-nineteenth century, my ancestors had undertaken an unknown journey to an unknown land. They were taken by the British from India as labourers under a system of indenture, contracted slavery, which had been created in order to maintain British fortunes in the colonies at the expense of human life and dignity.

As they were already living under the systemic impoverishment of life in India under British rule, it is unknown if they were coerced, kidnapped, or if they willingly boarded the ships in desperation that sailed from the ports of Kolkata (then Calcutta) and Chennai (then Madras) to the Caribbean and the north-eastern coast of South America.

They were taken to the sugar plantations in Guyana, to provide the labour that had previously been performed by Africans, whom the British had enslaved for two hundred years, when official slavery and its extended period of apprenticeship (slavery in disguise) was abolished in 1838.

Instead of freedom, the promise of wages and a better life, they found themselves bound to rigidly controlled and enforced labour, and they were cruelly used and abused to serve the hunger for power and the western cravings for sugar.

What were the pressures of forging a new life, and the restraints of the old, that filtered down through the generations? How much innate personal value was kept alive and fostered in the face of total control, threat, blame, and punishment and what compromises were made to survive and create a bearable life, let alone a happy one? What do you learn to concede of yourself in displacement and when can that concession be relinquished? How is loss of value, and fear of further loss, tolerated and balanced out to survive? How can the perpetual re-enactment be broken?

Intergenerational trauma may not be visible on the surface, but if we could see the thread of the scars of time then we could have the answers to these questions and we could see what we are striving to become free from. I think I knew from birth that control felt like suffocation, a separation from life itself.

Even as Guyana was moving towards independence in the 1950s, western powers sought to exert control by further entrenching racial, economic, and political division through violence and domination. It was in that climate of yet another form of deliberate disintegration of society by foreign powers, with the same intention as colonisation to disenfranchise, divide, rule and consolidate power, that many Guyanese left their country of birth. They emigrated mainly to North America and the United Kingdom, again seeking a better life.

One hundred years after my family's forced labour had been 'recruited' from India for Guyana, my father was recruited from the still British colonies to serve in the new British National Health Service. Not forced this time, but quite likely in an unfair and induced manner. I never heard his complaints, and I do not think he ever complained to those in authority, but I do recall my mother's consistent questioning over the years of our housing position, his income not being commensurate with his position, the lack of promotion, excess responsibilities given to him which he always undertook, and his chronic health conditions. My father's complaints took other forms.

My father qualified as a doctor in 1956, graduating from St Thomas's Hospital Medical School in England. In his training years, he frequently experienced the racist retort from sick patients, 'I don't want your black hands on me'. Black and brown hands were desperately needed, first for wealth and now for wellness. During these training years, my father developed loss of total body hair (alopecia universalis), and diabetes. His immune system was shattered, and his own body appeared to be turning on itself. Could these have been symptoms of a legacy of alienation and rejection? Maybe he could not tolerate life in England, because he went back to the Caribbean to practise medicine in Trinidad and on the small island of Tobago for several years. Both my brother and sister were born in Trinidad, but by 1961 he was exploring posts in England.

What compelled him to displace himself and family one more time? Unfortunately, I never had the answers from him, because generations of children were told not to ask questions. Everything was hush-hush with no accountability. We were told that we were brought to England for a better education, and it was education that broke the burden of indentured labour, but not the burden of diminished meaning and value. What was it my father was looking for and could not find? I never did find out. He died at the early age of 56 when his heart no longer supported him.

My mother felt deceived about coming to live in England, my father's contract was signed before she knew anything of it, and she did not recover from what she saw as a type of imprisonment in a foreign land. Neither did she forgive my father for bringing her here. Her own father had imprisoned her for wanting more freedom than he was prepared to give.

My mother had never been a free agent, she was bound or indentured to her father, then to her husband, and then to her own view of herself.

I am sure she suffered from culture shock and a deep

sense of loss of herself. We knew as children that there was always something missing in her life, and if it was missing in her, then by reflection it was missing in us. Within a year, she travelled from England to Guyana, pregnant with me, to reunite with my sister whom she had left as an infant with her parents. I believe she made the trip in the hopes of staying. It was a time when political and social instability had erupted in the form of strikes and riots, after persistent undermining by Britain and America of the country's efforts towards national unity and self-government. My mother did not want to return to England and probably not to my father, but she came from a very authoritarian patriarchal family where girls were expected to do as they were told and were held responsible for whatever happened, no matter what duress they had been put under. "If you make your bed you lie in it." Which really meant that you were responsible for others' actions against you.

There was blame and punishment for not conforming. You were cast out or shut in for not complying to the will of others. You would be left feeling that you were responsible for your disconnection, whereas in fact you had no free agency in the first place, no voice of equal worth. You were left with a constant feeling of being in the wrong and therefore you should be punished.

Our ancestors experienced it, my mother experienced it, I experienced it at her hands, and my daughter has experienced it at my hands. Repeating the pattern of the self-preservation strategy to separate, confine and control. But this strategy reflects a self-identity which is separated from its core, separated from its soul, separated from its true worth. The inner sense of separation gets projected onto life and others, creating our reality and validating what we feel, and so we are tricked into believing it rather than releasing it. Our only choice is perpetual re-enactment. And we do not tolerate anything that says any different because we are afraid to look beyond our own masks.

It is played out in society, in families, but first and foremost within our own mind-body system.

Both my mother and my father were imprisoned within their own minds, hearts, and bodies. How could that inner turmoil not be internalised by their children?

Born and Raised in the Riots

I was born in 1962 in Guyana, a country riven with the legacy of colonial rule, slavery, division, and conflict. It was a time of violent protests, as deep fears and insecurities of place and value erupted in society.

Despite this, the first six months of my life were probably when I felt the most at home in my surroundings and in my skin. From then on, my senses were disconnected, and it has been a tale of dislocation, and for many years, a near constant feeling of being uprooted, placeless and largely invisible. Out of family pressure, my mother returned to England with her three children at the beginning of 1963. In the first few months of being in England, I contracted pneumonia and was placed in a life-saving incubator in St Mary's Hospital in Eastbourne, where my father worked. I very nearly died.

Was I also experiencing my mother's sense of suffocation? The feeling of being smothered would stay with me for many years through nightmares of an inability to breathe or to move, and an overwhelming sense of dread and darkness. Vivid clouds of doom would suffocate me.

The air was not clear, it was polluted with fear and hatred, and I could not breathe. I was not entitled to breathe freely. I did not belong.

The move had taken us from a tropical summer to a severe northern winter and for many, many years, I remained cold from the inside out, never able to really feel warm. I never felt relaxed and protected in my own skin, in so many ways.

My parents are first cousins. They were given a dispensation from the Catholic bishops in Guyana to marry, as they were children of a brother and sister and not of two brothers. Whatever the parameters of the time, I do not think this was a wise decision. They each brought with them the compounded stresses and strains of the same family turned in on and against itself, with no escape. Double the effect, double the punishment. I think my father was happy in his work at the local hospitals, of which there were several that served the elderly in retirement and in convalescence, but he was a different man at home. These posts, of course, were the leftover posts that English doctors did not want to fill and some of the only ones that foreign doctors could apply for.

My mother was isolated and unable to find her voice,

her self-expression, and her sense of worth which had never been encouraged. She relied on her physical looks which had always been admired, and never ventured beneath the surface. She felt that she did not belong, that she had lost everything, and the message that came clearly from her was that we did not belong either. But what was really missing from both our parents was the deep internal feeling of being good enough and of self-acceptance.

My mother would often cry with a longing for something lost, and she was undoubtedly depressed and emotionally preoccupied and therefore unavailable for her children. It was a pattern I later repeated with my own children, having internalised my mother's sadness. Children feel their parents' pain, it reflects on them, giving the same messages of being incomplete.

My father was also absent as a parent, immersed in his work and never at peace at home. He did not engage with his children other than as pawns in a war game with my mother. Something was drastically missing from both their lives, which left a hole in the lives of their children. Outwardly, they blamed each other for their unhappiness, but inwardly they each carried the blame, shame, and guilt of their own sense of emptiness. This dynamic easily gets passed on to the next generation, finding its expression amongst the siblings.

Eventually however, I would find my freedom and wellness in the very town that *was renowned for its healing sea air and water, to which my father had brought us.*

As well as being born in conflict, I was raised in conflict. My experience of my family was one of suppression and depression, anger and violence, cynicism and bitterness. My father would become violently angry and either hit my mother or break things, or both. The arguments, the shouting, and the screaming were relentless. There was no reconciliation to speak of, instead everyone would go to their own corner to gather strength for the next round, including the children witnessing the events. My mother would bury herself in her cooking which became oppressive, as it would be forced upon us. It gave her meaning, and for a time it controlled her emptiness, at our expense. I do not recall happy times, just the familiarity of tension and conflict.

You could feel it in the air, and I grew accustomed to being able to smell the acridness of conflict coming.

When my father's fists rained down on my mother in front of our eyes, we would attempt to intervene if we could, or if it happened behind closed doors we would hold our breath until it stopped. Sometimes it would be my father smashing plates, destroying everything he could get his hands on for the time that his fury lasted. The kitchen would be littered with broken shards of crockery, every plate shattered. He aimed for and destroyed anything that had a meaning to my mother, including favourite ornaments and pictures taken from the walls. If he could destroy what mattered and belonged to her then he could destroy her, and her sense of belonging. This would include clothes and in later years he threatened many times to destroy my sister's and my clothes too. Was it because he felt destroyed and abandoned? His very sense of belonging taken away when his own father had left his family? Was he stuck in a trauma of loss, continuously replayed in his actions and through his physical health? His desperation could only be held in for so long before it would erupt from him again.

There was always clearing up to do. Clear it up, but do not talk about it. Clear it up as if it never happened. Clear it up, but do not challenge it. Clear it up and put it out of sight. That was the method, and for a long time it was my second nature, to just clear it up, clean it up and act as if it never happened. But of course, it kept happening over and over in front of my eyes and over and over when my eyes were closed. How do you really clear it up, how do you really clear the imprint that it has made, clear the stress that it has created? How do you go on untouched by it?

Can its effects be undone, can it be taken out of your soul and be replaced by the experience of true value that cannot be diminished?

We had to speak correctly and dress impeccably, especially when attending our local Catholic Church. I did not perceive a sense of guilt at church, there was enough of this at home. Instead, I felt a deep personal connection to an awareness, a truth that had no barriers. I associated it with Jesus, but it was beyond a name and form, how could it be limited? However, I soon found that the church was not a place of community, of freedom and belonging, but another hierarchical structure of control and subordination. My mother had spoken to our parish priest about the difficulties at home, which would have been out of sheer desperation, as these things were not usually spoken about with anyone outside the four walls that bore witness to what was enacted. The priest informed her that if she were to leave the abusive marriage, she would be excommunicated from the Catholic Church, which reinforced her responsibility, blame and punishment. She did not leave, but how I so desperately wished over the years that she would stop doing her 'duty' as she had been indoctrinated to do, so that we could all have a reprieve.

The message I received from my father was that I would stay at home and be someone's wife, and the message from my mother was that one day, I would rescue her.

Dark Clouds Closing In

I grew up during the time of the hate speeches of Enoch Powell. This was the very person who, as health minister, had recruited my father to serve in the newly formed National Health Service, and who then wanted to incite hatred against all those who had come to Britain. Was this another form of indentured service? Serve and do not aspire or claim to be equal and free? It was a repeated pattern of excommunication.

The phrase 'why don't you go back where you came from' has so often been repeated to me throughout my life. I grew up in the time of cowboy and Indian films, and I identified with the Indians who were always portrayed as savages. They had to be defeated and controlled and were seen as a threat to civilisation. I would have nightmares of the very same fights I saw on the television taking place in my own back garden, unprotected by the dilapidated fence at the bottom of it and the dangers of the jungle were brought to life. I was afraid I would be hunted down and captured, just as my ancestors had been ambushed into indenture. There was nothing to keep me safe, at home or in the world around me.

In the constant threat and eruptions of conflict, I could not afford to relax at home, and to grow in a carefree way and find my own expression. Instead, I was always on guard for when the next eruption would happen. As well as the nightmares that prevented me from sleeping, I was in a constant state of alert, listening to my mother's screams or listening to the quiet and having to stay awake to enjoy any respite available, waiting for the moment when I felt safe enough to go to sleep. I never felt safe.

Subsequently, I suffered from many years of severe sleep deprivation. Whenever I did sleep, I had the recurring nightmare of being suffocated by those familiar dark oppressive clouds. The only relief I could get was by locking myself in our blue and white tiled bathroom, crying for as long as I could, to get the darkness out of me. My parents were too absorbed in themselves to notice their children and to realise and protect their children's mental and emotional states.

Where we lived, we stood out for being well dressed. We stood out for speaking such good English. We stood out for not swearing. We stood out for working hard. We stood out for keeping quiet. But inwardly, we were wretched and wrecked.

A friend from my infant school wanted me to go to her house to play, so she said she would ask her mother. The next day she came back to school and told me that her mother said, 'we don't have Pakis in our house'. My friend did not understand it, and I did not understand it. I went home and told my mother who reinforced that we were not wanted. For some inexplicable reason, my friendship had limits and an invisible wall had been erected.

My mother would starch nearly all our clothes, a common Caribbean practice. At about twelve, I remember my hockey teacher laughing at my starched PE t-shirt. Why was something different to others yet normal to me, an object of ridicule? But when we went on school trips and could wear our own clothes or had mufti days at school, my clothes would be admired and as I had such nice outfits, I would be asked by my friends why I didn't go out with them after school. At that time there were youth clubs and discos, where it seemed like having the right clothes could also get attention and acceptance.

But when I asked my mother about attending events outside of school with my friends, I was told that I was not like them and that was not what we did, we did not mix in that way and that was the end of that. Echoes of what she had been told by her own father, that time in relation to African Guyanese. Clothes not only had their limits to fitting in or standing out, they were also designed to keep up pretences. The invisible wall was reinforced with no explanation that made any fundamental sense. There was no sense of rightness.

At thirteen, in a health and social education class, we

discussed belonging to a group. I had what I considered a good friend and several other friends, but I could not say that I belonged to a group, even though I could see that others clearly did or thought they did. The teacher could not accept this and admonished me for not conforming to the idea rather than teasing out what it might mean to belong to a group and what fundamental reality, if any, it was based on. It was one of the many failures in the educational system, and confirmed once again that I was in the wrong.

In the system, if you did not belong in an identifiable way, you must be wrong. Not only wrong, but a threat to the system.

I am not sure if we were one of the first Asian families in Eastbourne, but most of the time it felt like we were the only one. At school I was called 'curry' which I found absurd and annoying. My mother had befriended a Pakistani family, through my brothers' school, and we would regularly go to their home for tea. But when I saw them outside of the home, I pretended I did not know them or see them. I felt that if I did not recognise another brown outsider, then I would not be seen as a brown outsider. I was disowning a sense of myself and internalising not belonging.

I was becoming chronically stressed at home, and chronically tired, which created further stress. At some point, around the age of fourteen, my brain switched off. I was due to take an early GCSE exam in biology, which according to my academic history should have been a breeze. I remember trying to study for it alongside the battles at home, and my brain froze. How could I learn and focus when I was in a state of chronic stress and vigilance? My brain had been hijacked into operating in a perpetual survival mode, with no respite.

Being academically bright did afford some recognition and even admiration, along with the constant admiration of my long eyelashes and long hair. My academic ability was my point of connection with the world which I did not want to lose. I put myself forward for a school quiz while under this brain freeze. I knew I could do it, but my brain did not co-operate and I let the team down. My brain was only looking for a way to survive the constant state of stress. At this point, I moved firmly to the other side of that invisible wall of separation from the world.

My A level choices reflected my search to find the feeling of connection that seemed so elusive. My first choice was to study Latin, which I loved, because it seemed to contain beauty and clarity as well as philosophical investigation and discussion. But I was told it was a dead language and would lead nowhere. This message, whether consciously intended or not, was undermining and yet another personal devaluation. Opting for English, I was told that my writing was too abstract, and it seemed there was only reality on one side of the wall. I thought philosophy could explain this better, but there were no real discussions of ideas, only presumptions of certain ideas being real. I thought economics might explain interconnectedness in a different way, but rather than finding reason, I was shocked to find a startling belief in separation itself. A classmate whom I had considered a friend, told me and the class quite clearly on the prompt from the teacher posing the question "How would you feel if an Asian family moved in next door to you?", that he would be okay if it were me because he knew me, but not okay if it were anybody else whom he would consider a threat.

I could not believe that the teacher raised this question, commonly repeated in the 70s and 80s, without questioning the responses. I left the economics class learning that so many models in life are based on legitimising fear and determining strategies to manage a balance of fear of falsehoods, rather than promoting a balance of value. The devaluation of another and of self is not based on what is real. We see our own projected images of what is false, and no amount of projection makes it real.

Moving from an all-girls school to a co-education sixth form entailed an exposure I was not accustomed to. I had a crush on a boy, but kept it secret, for who was I to have any feelings? I went on a skiing trip and had my first romantic connection. When I got home, I was made the object of fun by my father and my brother, who questioned how I could be of interest to anyone. It left me completely devalued and I spent most of the next year putting on a huge amount of weight by eating incessantly. To set the table and serve was where I belonged, that was the message I received from the male members of my household. Yet there was still a streak of self-determination as I realised that I was not comfortable with the overeating and only I could change it, so I put myself on a strict diet and lost the weight very quickly. When I lost the weight, I also lost something within myself, my belief of connection to the world. Nothing made sense anymore, not even my love of mathematics. There was a huge wall in front of me, an invisible wall that was all too real. With no energy for life, I could not learn, and I was looking for an escape.

I had no help in navigating the internal pressures inside of me, and I do not think anyone noticed, certainly not my family or teachers, as they did not offer any assistance.

Was this part of the family legacy, that when the going gets tough you are on your own? From what had my family escaped when they left India and went to the sugar plantations of Guyana, which of course did not bring freedom but indentured slavery? Why had my family then escaped Guyana and moved to Britain which only brought isolation? Why did my mother have to escape from her own father who was ready to imprison her in order to control her, and why was I having to escape an alien world and a deep-rooted sense of not belonging and non-acceptance?

I went through the motions of my A levels and barely scraped a couple of passes. I was withdrawn and absent from college with my eyes set on my own escape plan, a teaching position at a secondary school under a voluntary service scheme in Kenya. I had opted to be placed at a project in Sri Lanka, but I was told that being Indian would be too confusing for local people as I would be too similar. Previously too different and now too similar, for what, to be equal? My friends thought I was either crazy or brave, but I was in fact just stressed and lost and my brain had already escaped. I played 'This land is for everyone' by the Abyssinians at a school assembly as I attempted to explain what I would be doing in the coming year. Playing it was more a plea for something that I did not feel.

I always cared about people in pain, and I wondered why care and attention were denied to so many. I was impatient with those who seemed to care about themselves, as it seemed self-indulgent and self-centred. When really, I was just in denial of my own existence. No one seemed to see, hear, care, or empathise with me. Was this the same anger that my father had felt and expressed so violently and that I would turn inward upon myself?

A Severed Life

When I went to Kenya, I had left home but I had not left the psychological and emotional ropes that bound and controlled me. On the face of it, I was successful in my teaching position at the community village school, and I enjoyed it.

But away from the familiarity of control of my family, the ropes of control became of my own making. How you are when you are alone with your feelings reflects a level of self-regulation, a negotiation between yourself, others and the environment. To find places of connection, reduce the heightened awareness of not feeling safe, and have an exchange of shared human value. I had not known this exchange, I had not felt entitled to this exchange, and I did not feel entitled to an existence. So, without the reflection of my family, the only sense of belonging I had, I was lost. I did not exist and had no right to exist.

*I controlled, blamed and punished myself,
and in doing so, I continued our family
legacy, a familiar torture.*

I did not have the inner resources to call on, because I was not shown any examples of how to be happy, and I did not have the teaching of a birthright to happiness. Instead it had been a lesson of not having rights, of not being allowed, of not having freedom of expression, of not knowing the love, care and protection that says you are okay; and even if it doesn't feel like it now, everything will be okay. When you are caught in the fear and the trauma you think it is anything but okay. How do you survive with the constant feeling of not being okay? It is acted out in vain attempts to bring a type of false relief to go on living, or sometimes to not go on at all.

My mother had developed great culinary skills and basked in the praise of her dishes. It felt like she lived for it, along with recognition of her beauty. But she was never engaged in conversation or asked how she felt. Under her guises of what she clung to for her own relief, we could not get close to her and so in turn felt rejected and never good enough. Cooking became what she was and feeding people became the means to matter. Eating showed recognition of her, not eating showed a rejection of her. I felt this pain acutely and knew that for her to be happy, my plate needed to be clean. I would eat everything she put on my plate to please her. I did not eat to satisfy myself and so in turn it became a reinforcement of rejection. I did not know that no amount of recognition can compensate for an internalised self-rejection.

At eighteen, with no secure internal attachment and away from home, I was unable to accept myself in a healthy way. Perversely, eating and sometimes not eating, had become an act of self-rejection. I continued in the same vein, with the only food that was available, a type of local fried sweet doughnut. I would eat as many as I could. They were starchy and sugary and gave a warmth, but this warmth was never enough, no amount was enough. There was a hole where I was supposed to be. Quickly the amount I ate became another oppressive feeling that I did not deserve to exist. I had become the void of not belonging.

My co-volunteer that I was living with described how she remedied her overeating by putting her fingers down her throat and making herself sick. The idea immediately took hold, then again and again. But it was not remedying overeating, it was reinforcing the feelings, the rejection, that overeating was displaying. The sense of worthlessness was compounded by the very act of purging.

Something had to be gotten rid of, and that something was me. It became a near daily occurrence in secret of course, after all it was blame, shame, guilt and punishment that I was re-enacting on myself.

Bulimia was a self-torture, a living nightmare that I was not waking up from. Back home my parents were as disinterested as ever, and I struggled to find anything that held a meaning. I did not see any point to life. It was a pain of non-existence, a suffering of a living death, and it hurt. Twice I tried to take my own life. The pills failed and I woke up, but the feeling of wanting to end my existence played out at other times. I was unhooked from my life. I was never asked how I felt or offered any help, but interestingly, it was then that my father gave me the second of his two statements of encouragement. He told me that people would listen to me. Since my suicide attempts had failed, I accepted that there had to be a reason for me still being here and I surrendered to that higher power and consciousness that I had felt to be real, albeit seemingly remote to me now. This transcendent power, as it had kept me here, had to show me the reason and the meaning. All I knew was that there was a purpose to my life and that purpose had to reveal itself as I was not able to break the self-destructive addictive habits of self-denial.

I accepted that some part of me was supposed to be here, a part that I did not know yet.

At the age of twenty-two, my mother packed a suitcase and handed it to me. That is how I knew I was leaving home. My parents could not tolerate my involvement with a man who was older, divorced, and English. I was naive and immature, unaware of what a healthy relationship entailed, unaware of what a healthy relationship to myself entailed. I became pregnant and felt a desperation to get married as a form of validation and legitimacy, out of the same intensity of pain of non-existence if I did not.

The stresses of being in an unhealthy relationship to myself as well as being in an unhealthy partnership with no real communication took its toll. "Why don't you understand, why don't you want to see or listen?" They were the repeated questions to my husband, even to my second husband in later years, but really to my own parents and by default to the world. "Why am I not good enough, why don't you accept me?" I was in an unhappy marriage, feeling alone, trapped inside my own head, not yet free from my own punishing relationship to myself.

Within three months of giving birth to my first child, I was pregnant again. Overwhelmed, already not present to myself or my baby, how could I have another when there was nothing left of me? I deliberately slipped down a long flight of stairs and miscarried. I wondered if my own mother had tried the same with me under the weight of depression. Regardless, I am sure she felt the same overwhelm and sense of oppression of 'I am not supposed to exist' in her life and that was reflected onto me. I conceived again eight months later, this time I was more present and it was planned. In the immediate period after the birth of my second daughter I was lost again in post-natal depression, invisible and overwhelmed. It eased after three months, but now with two children in a distant and disconnected marriage, I continued to feel isolated and desperate. A couple of years later I decided that the invisible wall could not be scaled, and I packed our bags and left.

And in the meantime, the bulimia continued, and every act of purging was an act of rejection. An act of not being present to myself and therefore not being present to my children. I was physically absent when the urge took over, and emotionally preoccupied with its near constant distraction of feeling absent from myself and in need. I thought tomorrow would be different, but it never was, the days ended the same way, in defeat and more shame, and that deep internalised blame for every act of need that was met by self-punishment.

Breaking the Walls

I started to realise that I could not escape. I couldn't escape the absence that I felt, or escape the overwhelm of not feeling whole. The escape plan was not working. But it never does, we just reinforce its narrative. What kind of life was it to be in constant avoidance of yourself, feeling that you are void or trying to pretend and insist that you are not?

I knew that burying myself was not an answer and I wanted answers. I wanted the answers to my freedom. Was there something real to be present to?

From that point on, I knew I had to embark on a more active search to find freedom from my own perspective of pain and non-existence. My focus would be to find what was beyond myself, to be free from the ideas of me in my mind and in my acting out. I had heard stories of an uncle who was ridiculed and discredited for going on a spiritual quest in search of his true self, but now I started to wonder what he might have found.

I had to start reaching for the answers, to be in pursuit of and to reclaim the truth of my existence, to stop being a victim of my own ideas of myself and anyone else's idea of me. I could sense that this reclamation required me to be free from not only the me that I had come to know and re-enact, but also from any other idea of me which could only be equally untrue even if it appeared to be a better version. It could not be a true me, no external definition could be.

What am I without a defining form, any defining form? I did not want to swap forms, whether it be in this life replacing one addictive habit or identity with another, or in my next reincarnation attached to a different form of me, I wanted to know what was behind all changing forms.

The search for the substance of this true self, an inner, unknown, non-dependent and unconditionally whole self, gathered momentum over the next twelve years.

It was a pursuit, not to acquire but to become free from the constant noise within myself that was controlling me, the unconsciousness of hijacked attention.

I knew that my actions were not born out of true choice, rather they were a result of internalised false information diverting me. It was evident that I gained only fleeting relief in the moment and it became apparent how self-destructive my habits were. I was wrecking my immune system, compromising my natural processes and resources, but the most subversive driver was my own mind and the way it was holding a fixed and unchanging view. Classic symptoms of stress overload and the locking in of the fight or flight survival response to it, blind to all else. But how do you break the hold of repetitive habits and the thoughts that drive them, to unbury yourself from the false meanings you have constantly reinforced?

It started with being present to myself, a conscious decision to acknowledge what I was doing with acceptance, without judgement, to not turn away in shame, blame, or guilt. A meditation on myself, an observation in a relaxed way, instead of a diversion in an overstimulated reactive and threatened way. It meant that I could start to be present to a me that was beyond my actions and more than my actions. I did not have to wait to feel differently about myself when or if I acted differently tomorrow, I was here now despite myself. I was behind it, beyond it somehow, but always present, not somewhere else at some other time. The more acceptance I showed myself, the more I felt a truer and deeper relief. The less I was defined by my actions, the more my actions changed, the more I moved beyond the programming and the more I started to feel my own real presence, a peace, a calm, a joy.

My attention, or rather my awareness, was now on this presence of being and wanting

*to further discover it. I started to feel a
fullness which left a deeper impression than
the emptiness.*

This fullness was richer, self-comforting and unconditional, and it broke the bulimia. There was more space between episodes, their intensity reduced with less and less power and momentum, then stopped. It had burnt out and something else, more available, and more fulfilling was growing stronger and drawing me.

I particularly started to enjoy the space and relief that nature provided and engaged in more physical activity, which had not been encouraged when I was younger. The bulimia had carried on for many years and its negative feedback ended as I forgave my parents for not being present, stopped blaming them and stopped blaming myself. It was also about the time when my daughters were the age that my own decline had begun.

I embarked on a soul education, self-led with the determination to find unconditional truth in the here and now, to be present to being, not influenced by meanings accumulated from the past. Present to myself in the way that my first teacher had been to me, who had never blamed me, even when I let the budgerigars out of their cage, and they escaped from the classroom.

*Unlearning and erasing my own
survival strategies, coping mechanisms,
rationalisations and storytelling, the self-*

painted picture, and the addictive habits of chronic stress management.

Having been cut off from a sense of well-being, from my own mind and body, I started to reconnect and search for what true and unconditional connection was. Bringing up children while you are trying to bring up yourself is a constant challenge, and I made mistakes even as I started to learn. But the lingering shadows, the unconscious ghosts of my own experiences were still attached to me, how could I shake them?

I took parenting classes. I read every book on the self-development shelf of my local library. I enrolled in a counselling training course and received counselling, but was not advised to keep my feelings and insights to myself.

When parents do not fully take responsibility for their children's security, it becomes beholden on the children to create their own strategies of meaning for their survival, to make the pieces fit together somehow, and then they must defend those meanings for their continued sense of safety. It can sometimes lead to attacking each other's patterns of meaning. Either way, it is a rationalisation of disconnection instead of a pattern of connection imprinted upon them.

I wanted to discover healthy resources and connections, but also to investigate and go through and beyond the limits of those very resources, physically, mentally, and emotionally, to find out what was beyond. The ultimate relaxation from thinking, feeling, and acting, because any thought, feeling, or action can only be partial, and I wanted the whole. I knew the master formula held all partials together, as the perfect impartial. I wanted to stretch myself, to break myself open and find the connecting fabric of life beyond every thing, every form, and everyone. To find the uncompromised, the undivided.

I worked through physical, psychological and emotional modalities to uncover and explain that elusive fabric. I trained in movement therapy, psychotherapy, hypnosis, and martial arts. All to break down the limiting forms of dependency, identity and reveal the bigger, truer and unconditional reality that was behind it all.

Gradually, it felt like a picture was emerging but still there was no clear experience of the nature of this picture. I had not become it yet.

I started working with families of young offenders in the criminal justice system, on generational patterns of trauma, emotional neglect, psychological defence mechanisms, and addictive survival strategies. These family patterns and systems were having an impact and were reflected in the wider social systems. Connections had turned into division, peace into violence, the one against the self, the one against the other, or the many against the many, it was the same pattern of fragmentation occurring on all levels. I wanted to know not just the cause, but the remedy, as the effects were all too obvious and the pain, suffering and despair all too real and familiar. I had the examples in my own life, the brokenness, discord, and an unhealthy damaging rhythm repeated and played out over generations.

What is the lasting remedy for the fear of separation and non-existence that the survival mechanisms of fear, fight or flight enact and operate in so much of our lives? What is the true connection of existence beyond any and all frames of reference and how is it found? What new system and intelligence can, and does, govern us that is not polarising?

Rhythm was in my blood, I was acutely aware it held all expression, sweetness and sorrow. I knew rhythm could speak of freedom, of healthy awareness and flow that could spiral outwards as gently as petals unfolding yet as powerful as waterfalls. I had felt it through my love of dance and my love of water both through which I could experience a rhythm of purity and connection. They brought something to life.

I could relax in water, I could feel dissolved of any sense of self or non self and still be. I could relax in the flow of dance without restrictive boundaries. I could feel the possibility of being the flow rather than the frame in the flow.

But how can the rhythm and vibration of my frame truly come into harmony with the flow of vibrations of universal connection, of oneness and wholeness and what is the vibration of the rhythm of life?

It never made sense that one thing could not be connected to another, even though I had felt its pain, yet something prevents this reality from being perceived and experienced.

Was pain the fear of something that was not true?

How insidious it is that fear of what is not true can be so easily perpetuated. How much more powerful then must truth be, aware of itself with no space for fear.

By now I had also found a rhythm in practising chi kung which gave me a connection to a constant inner flow. It gave me a different language through which to speak to myself just as any practice of the spirit does. The chi kung teacher was a true practitioner of the spirit having learnt his art in China and he spoke of healing energy. He introduced the class to the writings and visions of Paramahansa Yogananda, an Indian yogi who taught in the west. I felt an instant connection and recognition.

By the time my daughter turned fifteen, she had become estranged from me, and I seemed to be losing her. It was an excruciatingly painful time, and I did not know where to turn, all my resources were drained. A personal relationship had also just ended, which had been physically and emotionally intense and I was feeling the pain of separation again.

Why were my connections breaking down, especially to my child which was an almost unbearable type of loss? Where should I look for answers and relief, and to put it right, which I so desperately wanted to do?

It is only a true friend who is brave enough to direct you back to yourself, to get you to look within to see what obstacles you are holding within your own perceptions, to bring you out from your suffering.

They can help you realise that it is not and does not have to be what it seems, for you to break through the internal walls of built-up scar tissue, to find a different reality from within. I had such a good friend, who at this time of personal crisis gave me a method to do it, and I was prepared to do anything. At this point, you also must be brave enough or desperate enough to break your own shell, but there really is no other choice for true and lasting change.

My friend introduced me to the Buddhist chanting practice of Nichiren Daishonin. Based on the core chant Nam-myoho-renge-kyo, distilled from the Lotus Sutra of Gautama Buddha's teachings on karma. It breaks the spell of believing in a fixed reality and liberates a different sense of self from that suffering, a different vibration of self. This higher vibration of self imparts to you a knowing and experience of the joy of your existence. It asks in mutual recognition for the awakening of the highest vibration of self in others and takes you out of conflict mode.

I was committed to the practice because I wanted desperately to change my experience and I knew that meant I had to change myself. That I was the one that needed to change. I had to stop trying to change everyone and everything else. My feelings and experiences were dependent on me alone and not the cause of anyone else. I believed I could change, that I could be connected to a different reality, a different reality of me. I practised with sincerity and found an almost instant relief from the burden of my own identity. I was back in the joy of my infant school experience.

I wanted to thank everyone in my life for giving me the opportunity to see me, for helping me to turn back to and get in touch with that uncorrupted self that can arise, just as a lotus rises out of the murky waters and is untouched by it. I felt a greater depth of love and compassion for all, especially my daughter and myself.

The outcome was the stated purpose of the process, unimaginable to the mind but as clear and simple as daylight and the freedom to breathe.

All of my life's circumstances, now with the first vibrational energy formula, was to set the stage for what was to come and the further collapsing of my walls.

The Unleashing

As I started to feel the relief of pressure on my heart and in my mind, the physical symptoms of being sick with worry and panic abated, and I became more hopeful of a change that had a truer, deeper, and richer quality, of unmined resources.

It was clear that it was my own internal reactions that caused me pain, and I wanted to be free from that. I was longing for things to be made right, to find peace and relief from my thoughts and feelings, to be free from the meanings I had attached to them. I longed to be in acceptance without struggle, ultimately free within myself, from myself, and the internal stress and pressure that it had created. I wanted connections to be rebuilt, for walls to be removed, for doors to be reopened, for voids to be filled and new meanings found. I wanted the inseparable truth behind all the different and changing ideas of what is real, of what I am and what you are, of what I need, of what I am not. I wanted to overcome the rigidity of restrictions that disrupt the interconnectedness and flow of life.

I wanted the all-pervasive truth that I had sensed and always knew must exist beyond the all-pervasive cloud.

The surrender to be released from my own self-identification, grew stronger as if taken on a wave with its own momentum in a perfect storm of pressure. It was a wholesome pressure rather than a divisive pressure of desire to hold onto some blinkered meaning and desperate attachment. An unstoppable freedom instinct subsumed the fear-based survival instinct. This pressure was a gathering of energy, a conflagration of my constantly re-enacted beliefs, transforming the walls of my thoughts and actions into primordial streams of flowing vibration. The internal call to action and to truth had been sounded. It was a mass attesting of energy, a swarming towards a deep internal re-unification.

Gone was the feeling of being lost and denied, a pressure squeezing from the outside in, the inability to breathe, the weight in the heart, the knot in the stomach. Instead, the growing life-force was emerging from the inside out, it came and was determined from within me, and gathered at a precise centre of location in my body. Discomfort transformed into the most profound reassurance of truth, a warm rotating energy at the base of the spine, building, spreading itself and pushing outward, further and further through me. As well as being multi-directional and multi-dimensional, it rose upwards and along my spine into my head. An internal explosion of energy, a super-charged rocket to infinite space, an overpowering and all-consuming dynamic flow. It blew my bodily sense of being. At times I would feel my spine physically elongate as the subtle energy was unleashed through the spinal column.

Beyond the speed of light, it struck like lightning, with clarity, power, beauty, warmth and truth, it spoke of love, of oneness, of nothing other than it.

The pure, total and tangible potential behind everything, the one constant, the formation of everything, the formless of every form, that which is the substance of giving life, taking life, and changing life, and which is itself unchanged. Self-perpetuating creation power. It said that everything was made of this and nothing and no-one was separate from it. There is no other thing and no other one to be or not to be, to fear.

It first happened whilst doing the chanting practice and continued every time I chanted but also occurred at other times and just recalling it would be enough to ignite it again. It was a power unto its own about which I had no doubt, and it was fun to marvel at the game it played by its own rules, in control and uncontrollable.

Other internal sensory symptoms arose quite rapidly, generated of their own accord by the internal stimulus.

The sound of a thunderous hum between my ears, an internal sweet smell like nothing I have smelt with my nose, and an internal taste beyond anything I had tasted, a smell and taste of the pure power of peace and love. These sensory perceptions were giving me information about an internal reality, and it was a reality that had no defining limits. It was an infinite landscape.

I started to recognise that it was alerting me as a signal, an internal signifier of truth, of something or someone near or far that was in resonance with truth, openness and authenticity. It was the sensation of truth itself, the feeling of the vibration of pure flow, pure connectedness recognising itself. It told me what was real and what was not. It also signified change when it was acting to disconnect a closed system of fear and bring about the re-establishment of truth. It was the fabric of reality that originates from within and reveals itself from within. Everything was turned inside-out, external reality was more and more abstract, less tangible as I had always suspected, it was just an idea and one that could be changed.

I realised that primarily, reality was based on the falseness of fear.

External perceptions were changing, my internal reality was more reliable than my external reality and a divide seemed to be opening between the two. I was disappearing into that divide. My body perception decreased, I also lost a dramatic amount of weight and felt a sense of non-body existence. The walls of differentiated existence came down.

I had to be careful how I spoke to those around me, as I spoke of what our ordinary senses could not perceive, impressions not bound by the mind's limited faculties that are based on survival of a form. Seeing into the infinite depths of the sky and feeling its embrace, the sky was my best friend, as we were one and the same.

I had to stop the chi kung practice as it would overstimulate the energy and make it impossible for me to keep my feet on the ground, and at one point the instructor tried to help by throwing me to the floor. I became most comfortable in an inverted position as gravity was now in sync with the flow of energy from the base of my spine to my head. I had to be careful of driving and limited my distances. I had to avoid bright lights and loud noises as these would oppose and disturb the peaceful flow of this current which I instinctively knew was at work in its own space and time and was its own world. There was nothing more precious. It was as if I was being cocooned, sheltered and protected and I knew that it was what I had always been looking for, that I could trust it and it would give me answers.

I wanted to know it more, to understand it more, know what it was for and what it could do. This life force, with an intelligence of its own, had to have a purpose and if it could have such a purifying de-personalising and liberating effect on my life, then surely it could have an impact for others.

I began to hear information, experience a clarity

devoid of words, and see intricate geometric patterns. I was being deconstructed and simultaneously reconstructed from the inside out, rebuilt and remodelled. It was not me having a new experience, but a new experience of me, without the ability to identify with myself or hold on to any idea of me.

In its place something more real was taking shape with more freedom from the grief of the old mould.

What did I need to do to understand this force of creation?

I tried to find anyone with a personal experience of it who could answer some questions and give some guidance, but I could not find anyone who had a direct personal experience. The closest I came was through a book recommended by a yoga teacher, who recognised the signs and symptoms but could not instruct me further. He pointed me in the direction of Gopi Krishna's writings on his experiences of kundalini awakening, which confirmed the phenomenon. I did not have the contra-indications that he described, mine really was a smooth passage. I believe this was due to being prepared to let go of my own ideas about myself, a surrender not of life but of holding on to my form of being me. To anyone else that I spoke to it was clear that they not only had no experience but little true awareness of this power or its meaning.

Here was the non-duality of energy. Pure vibrant undifferentiated power that is at the heart of all forms.

Kundalini actively takes back all attachment to form and therefore all fear of being a separate form, removing the block between the natural and supernatural energy flow.

I carried on searching and investigating over the next couple of years. Ancient Indian texts described the nature and awakening of kundalini but only in a supernatural way, not a purposefully active way. Modern western writings described it only in a physical person-centred context.

I knew the person-centred approach was not accurate, but at the same time it was a human experience of the supernatural.

I read more spiritual books. These books described the meaning and fundamental purpose of life. I read esoteric books about the nature of existence, including 'Autobiography of a Yogi' by Paramahansa Yogananda which my chi kung teacher had introduced me to. This book always faced outward on my bookshelf because the cover photograph of Yogananda bore a striking resemblance to my mother. That is how I saw it and it drew me in. Most of what I read made sense, but I wanted a greater understanding of the supernatural mechanisms and their purpose for me. I was having the supernatural energy experiences of the current of creation, but what was the purpose in the supernatural mind of creation? I continued to ask for this internally and intentionally.

The Presence

I no longer attended the Catholic Church, but I never went to bed without making the sign of the cross and speaking to what I believed to be a universal presence. Now I knew the energy of this presence more intimately, I wanted the walls between natural and supernatural awareness taken down.

As much as I liked to read, I also liked to sit. In silence, especially in the morning, before daily activities and work started. I liked to just be still and quiet and I had a regular chair by the window in which I sat. I also looked forward to sitting in that chair in the quiet at the end of the day. There was more reality and reassurance in silence than in activity. Silence was full, undivided, and open.

There were no walls in silence and this chair became my doorway into a space of deep relaxation and sense of completeness.

Beside my chair was a carved wooden head of Buddha. A couple of years earlier, I had visited ancient rock caves in Sri Lanka. I was drawn into one that was not on the tour, it was disused and near abandoned. Inside, I saw a huge sculpture of a laying down Buddha and in that moment I disappeared. I did not exist in that time or space. When I was back in the cave and then went outside, I realised that everything else going on was in a different reality. Still, I wondered why no-one else was going into that cave. The experience of being out of the form of time and space re-occurred, this time in full awareness and presence.

As I sat in my chair by the window that night, there seemed to be a rapid acceleration into the fullness, not the usual slow and calm pace I had grown accustomed to and comfortable with. There was a momentum out of my control, one that I could only witness. I was fully awake and cognizant of what seemed to be an internal experience whilst completely aware of my surroundings. I opened and closed my eyes several times just to check, but it made no difference, the experience continued.

I had no idea what was happening, I could not hold onto any idea, my mind did not have a grasp. I was being sucked into the space, disappearing. I could see my body, but I was simultaneously vanishing, I was losing all appearance to myself, as myself. I was about to die. There was nothing I could do voluntarily or involuntarily. I had nothing to hold onto, I could not go back, I could not resist. I was slipping away extremely fast and with a moment of fear, a recognition of death, of no longer being.

But I was being embraced by, and dissolving into an immense and inconceivable power. I was gone. I did not exist.

And simultaneously I was present. I had gone through the dark night of death and found an existence beyond all time, not as me, but as existence itself. No identification to mark me out in time. I was present outside of time, awareness itself without form.

In the darkness and the space where I had no body and no identity, I was the space itself and the witness of that space, the constant presence. Peaceful, beautiful, serene, complete, pure awareness. There was no me and at the same time I was the perceiver of everything as me. In this space of everything being one, there is no space for what is not, the perceiver, perception and the perceiving are as one, nothing other, more or less, everything itself and itself everything. This dark night was the counterpart to the energetic experience of kundalini, the consciousness of self where no separate or individual self exists, only the consciousness of creation as itself. It blew my mind wide open.

Here was the non-duality of consciousness. Pure undifferentiated awareness, which frees all sense of identity in time and space.

This non-identified reality merged with my body awareness. I had died and I was still here, sitting in my chair in my home, and now the two states had to coexist.

The formless creation-consciousness with the body-mind form, east and west, supernatural and natural as one.

When I regained some sense of time, forty-five minutes had passed. Forty-five minutes for life and death to merge into one state and the reality of creation to be born.

Now I had the sensory and conscious perception of no 'I', a union of body and mind with creation. How can this union which liberates the suffering of the 'I' as me, be known to many? As I was shedding deep internal layers of angst and agitation, I wanted to know how these experiences could be translated to others. How could the walls of so many I-and-other projections be broken? How could the true power behind any and of all forms be known in any form?

I wanted to know how to really help others be free from the wall of fear that binds and blinds. Above all, I wanted the formulas, the energy-consciousness formulas of this freedom, for the transformation and disruption to the perpetuation of division.

I came to learn that my 'death' experience was a speedy and astronomical experience of the dark night of the soul, a spiritual rite of passage. Again, I believe mine was smooth as I was prepared for the surrender, asking for the false layers of self-identification to be removed. Over the next few months, I read more about supernatural phenomena and spiritual phenomena, and there were many descriptions, but no clear connection between the experience, awareness of that experience, and purposeful implementation. I read Nisargadatta Maharaj's 'I Am That' explaining consciousness of non-duality, as I had read Paramahansa Yogananda describing the energy experiences of non-duality and I had my own experiences of both.

Now I wanted to find the bridge that would show how this freedom could be passed on, address the human condition of suffering and halt the passing on of fear.

I knew that my experiences were bigger truths, meant for more people than just for me, that there was a power that could bring about change and I wanted it to reach many. For others to experience the relief, freedom, deep peace, connection and belonging that I had experienced. For relationships to be mended, just as my relationship with my daughter had been mended. For what is true to be known. It was my aim to open a healing centre for people to receive healing from trauma, personal, generational, and collective, just as I had received through my spiritual experiences. I wanted to raise the power of freedom that is innate and infinite within everyone, to be truly and fully informed by what is within, to overcome any wall of definition that tries to separate, be it in body, mind, or heart. I felt that my experiences needed to be formulated.

I tried to do some more exploring, but I had explored everything I could find in England that might shed further light. I could not find a big enough frame of reference. Instinctively, I knew that I had to create some space and that what I was looking for would emerge from that space, much like the silence and the experiences that had come from it. So, in 2005, in order to create this space, I requested and took a three-month sabbatical from my job.

Answers of an Avatar

Almost immediately after taking this break, another good friend, a soul friend, showed me an advertisement for a visiting Indian guru coming to London to give a public talk. His name was Sri Sai Kaleshwar, and he was from Penukonda, Southern India.

As soon as I looked at the ad and read the information on his website, I knew that he had the answers I was looking for. He was talking about healing the pain of suffering, freedom from illusion, knowing the ultimate reality of life, and particularly realising our connection to the one power and source of creation, our Creation Mother. And all of this had been encapsulated in formulas that he was sharing.

He was giving out the codes to unlock the mysteries of fundamental questions that nothing else could answer, the codes of my very own experiences, and the means by which they could be passed on to others. These codes had been passed on from creation through avatars, who were liberated souls who make the bridge between the supernatural and the natural.

They bring the answers to liberation, especially in the darkest of times, to show us the methods that take us back home to the power and truth within us, to end our ideas of division.

I went to London to hear Sri Sai Kaleshwar speak, and then I travelled to India to his ashram in Penukonda a few weeks later. It felt like a natural pull, like the pull of gravity to the power and information of creation energy at its core.

During my first conversation with Sri Kaleshwar, whom I refer to as Swami, while sitting by his sacred fire-pit at the ashram, he asked me many questions. He asked what my concerns were, which he listened to one-by-one. I told him about my family, about how my mother had numbed her pain with alcohol for so many years, and about wanting a healing centre. He told me to learn the techniques, then he said slowly "I see you have the energy, I see you have the energy. I will train you personally". Never before had anyone understood what I had only ever cautiously alluded to, that was running through my spine, let alone seen it. So, my first reaction was to think that he was speaking metaphorically.

Later, I realised he was literally seeing the current of energy within me with his eyes, and that he not only recognised it, but would train me how to use it. It was the greatest relief. I knew he had the formula for it and that its purpose was the healing of suffering. He added in a very casual way, "I have been watching you for eighteen months", and I knew instinctively that he had been watching me through the eyes of Yogananda on the cover of 'Autobiography of a Yogi'. Swami sent me to the Jesus Temple and the training began. It was now early January in 2006.

I had the desire to know myself and my purpose, to change my family's problems, and the strongest desire to help others. In the seconds that it took to let Swami know what I wanted, he wiped away the feelings of desperation of having to find answers, to make something happen, and the perception that I determined anything. Instead, praying in the Jesus Temple, I felt all my concerns rest and relax in that loving energy, and I knew that everything was answered and granted. At last, I was okay, and everything was okay. I did not have to worry and was overwhelmed with relief in that knowing. There was no longer any division between the supernatural and the natural. Everything was possible, made possible by a supernatural truth beyond form and of form itself, real and responsive. Love was in control, forgiving the notion that anything could be other than it.

I wanted this power of love in action to flow everywhere.

Before meeting Swami, I had already become

accustomed to thinking and asking deeply about what troubled me and what I was really looking for. I had found there was always a form of fear in any desire and what I was asking for always entailed being released from that. Fear is the hidden face of desire and I wanted to get to the place beyond fear, to get to the point. The point beyond desire, and the point beyond time that manifests desire.

It became natural to speak to Swami in this way. I would filter my questions down to one or two points, filtering out fear as much as possible, to ask for the nuggets of truth beyond any personal desire, and rehearse them so they were clear. It was an especially useful habit because he wanted his students to recognise what they were holding and be honest as well as forgiving of themselves.

His answers would always be to wash out any remaining fear, then open the supernatural channels of power that dispel fear.

These distilled questions, distilled to the point where you are not asking anything for yourself, are no longer or are in less fear for yourself, became a way of connecting to Swami, a hook that he invariably took. He would call me over and ask what I wanted as well as giving me whatever information and instruction he wanted to give. One day, he asked me in the familiar way that people in India will always do, which part of India my family was from. I told him that an aunt had traced our family to one of the northern states of Uttar Pradesh. This would have been likely as the vast majority of the indenture ships sailing to the Caribbean had left from the eastern port of Kolkata, taking people from the Central and Northern Provinces. But Swami shook his head and pointed to the ground, saying "here, you are from here". I was surprised and thought he must be referring to my reincarnated soul history rather than to my bloodline. As with so many things that Swami said, it can take some time for the real meaning to become clear. But again, he was speaking literally, and sometime later I realised that he was in fact referring to my direct bloodline, that he could see my family history.

He could see my lineage with all the fears and desires and suffering that it carried.

I had come full circle. Some of my family had lived in southern India, they were Telugu speaking people who had been recruited and boarded the ships at the southern port of Chennai. More precisely, they had come from Penukonda in the Anantapur district of Andhra Pradesh state. Only five per cent of the Indians taken to the Caribbean were from the southern Tamil or Telugu speaking regions. I was returning approximately 160 years later, but it was not about a physical homecoming, it was a coming home to the existential answers I had been seeking.

Home is where the heart is, where the soul is, where

the answers to yourself lie. Home is where you know who you are, where you can breathe and be sustained because you know you belong and are not separated. These answers were the deepest and most profound universal answers to belonging, beyond all history and forms of existence and separation, beyond all identity, to the power beyond.

This self-inherent power of belonging was first cognized in Penukonda by ancient sages and seers many thousands of years ago. It was revealed by creation itself through vibrational sound (mantra) and pattern (yantra). Given as a soul map, it provides a route to short-cutting karma and leads back to the heart of creation. The ancient knowledge had been passed on orally and then inscribed in palm leaf manuscripts, preserved energetically, reawakened and passed on when the need and time was right.

Now Swami was passing on these formulas of mantra and yantra to awaken our divine innate nature of love and belonging. He was bringing western students to his ashram, and it became increasingly apparent that it was for the meeting of two mentalities. To merge the eastern surrender to and awareness of the formless power behind all forms with the western drive of seeking to be informed by that power and experience it.

Merging hemispheres, mentalities, archetypes, and subtle energy channels for the power to flow as one breath, one heart, one home.

Shirdi Sai Baba, a saint and master of non-attachment to form, already out of his own form, trained Swami and passed on the formulas for him to teach the merging of consciousness of non-duality with the power beyond all form. To merge true meaning with right action, for right action to bring us home to true meaning, to teach us to practice and be patient. I did not have to be a saviour or a slave as per my parents' expectations, I could have a different life experience, one of freedom.

After this first visit of two weeks, Swami asked me to come back to the ashram in a couple of months, which I managed to do only shortly after returning to work. The inevitable happened and he asked me to stay. I knew at this point that I had to resign from my job. Finding the answers had been the purpose of my life. That was my job.

Three months later, Swami started the Soul University with just over one hundred students at the ashram. I enrolled on a part-time basis, with the intention to attend for three months and be back home in England for one month. It never happened that way, as Swami would invariably ask me to prolong my stay or return earlier to the ashram. Over the course of the year, I undertook intense spiritual practices and processes, personally directed by Swami.

Years of trying to change my troubled teenage daughter turned in a moment to profound recognition of herself as me, me as herself. This was the key to liberation, a reflection of pure oneness. Years of trying to change my chronically heartbroken mother, turned on the eve of her death to a time where no pain or problem existed, there was no issue left to talk about, no separation of our hearts. There was a serene comfort in the flow of life, helping me to realise what truly already exists, what does not need to be struggled for and what cannot be fought for. It was an extraordinary blessing to experience that oneness as a mother with my daughter, and as a daughter with my mother, problems that I had sought to change dissolving in the union, and the knowledge I had sought of myself springing from it.

One more time, Swami asked me to stay longer than I had planned, to show me the truth.

One day, I was standing on the balcony on the fourth floor of the students' apartment building, looking out to the hills beyond, when in an instant everything I could see was under water. Then just as suddenly, the water literally parted before my eyes. The water that was covering everything parted in the middle, like an ocean opening from its depths and receding on either side. Waves curled back on either side. Immediately, I knew this was the parting of the sea that Moses and his followers had witnessed.

It was not a metaphor, but a spiritual mechanism of coming out from the illusion of suffering.

A coming out from, or a crossing of the waters, which reflect all illusion of experience. Crossing the waters of our own and our collective illusion of who and what we think we are to experience a different reality, a different reality brought to life. This was the power, the life-force made visible, the great angel of the waters parting the veil.

The veil of dark clouds, the hauntings of personal, family and society's dispossession and punishment, hurt and hate, were erased, transported and filtered out of my consciousness. Water had always been close to my heart and now I knew why. It had the ability to wash out from consciousness, bring into consciousness, or change the picture of our consciousness stuck in our minds. All traditions that value the sacredness of water recognise that it helps us to see and know ourselves more clearly, but we cannot have this clarity when the waters are polluted with fear.

Swami was answering my questions through experiences and giving me the formulas through all the prescribed practices and the mantras of vibrational codes to change reality. He was showing me that to overcome the pain of our deepest fears of extinction, we need the existential energy of freedom to wash out our fears.

I had surrendered to freedom, I was informed by freedom and now I was learning the techniques, the formulas to implement freedom.

Bringing out From Beyond

The teachings in the Soul University began with the energy system of the origin of life and the means to connect with that pure energy. To purify ego, desires, and fears that lead us further and further away from our true nature of being that one source. To take us home, home to our centre of power and clarity that is creation itself. This is the teaching of the Holy Womb Chakra which operates particularly dynamically in women.

This master chakra (subtle energy wheel) is the operating centre from where our life starts, runs, and ends, and it connects us to all lives and all of life.

It is the source from which all nadis (subtle energy nerves) stem. Women have this channel of connection, this interconnected web of connection, and can implement its power to reveal connection and heal separation, to destroy ego and not one another.

Swami initiated and taught ancient supernatural healing mechanisms relentlessly. Spiritual processes involved learning mantras and yantras, fire ceremonies, studying ancient knowledge and encrypted energy formulas from palm leaf manuscripts, and long hours of meditation. A particular focus was power objects, and how the power and clarity of the Holy Womb Chakra, of pure undivided supernatural connection, can be transmitted through the natural elements, then be received.

Penukonda itself had been created as a huge power object, a power spot for the transmission of divine energy. It is where the channels of the Holy Womb have manifested in the natural world. A ground which has held the secret and sacred knowledge for millennia and has now released its power and supernatural mechanisms to the world.

Transmission of this power is a sacred process, requiring deepening internal development, discipline, and remodelling, on the part of the initiate. The tools are practise, patience, surrender, openness, sincerity of intention, love, faith, and following precise formulas; all with a willingness to suspend thoughts, beliefs, and habits, to question what we hold as fact. Bringing our attention in, putting our own actions and reactions on hold, and challenging our own self-perception is critical for a new, bigger perception to be revealed. The new picture emerges from within and is then born into the world, seen internally then made visible externally. This new reality, or creation, is an expression of the one universal beating heart.

Supernatural energy-consciousness stirs and forms deep within the silence, beyond the nature of the mind-body system. This super-power can be brought to life and birthed in many ways.

It is a formless universal reality born to dismantle the forms of falsehood of a separated self.

I witnessed two supernatural births, eighteen months apart, and these supernatural energy forms were delivered into my hands.

The birthing of a lingam is a little-understood supernatural phenomenon. It mimics the birthing of human life where the parents', particularly the mother's, own energy goes into its formation. In this case, it is the reproduction of a saint's energy with the consciousness of that saint, the birthing of pure life-force itself absent of ego. I refer to saint here as someone who has access to the highest cosmic channels of healing, of changing creation.

The birthing of a lingam is a self-born re-creation that takes the form of an oval or egg-shaped stone which grows in the stomach and then at exactly the right time, is birthed through the mouth. It is normally black, and its purpose is to pass on those channels of healing as it emanates the consciousness and life-force of the soul that gave birth to it.

On both occasions the stone, the lingam, was slightly softer to the touch initially upon birth then hardened as a rock.

The first to give birth to a lingam was the widely recognised Indian saint, Shirdi Sai Baba. This saint left his human body in 1918 and the birth was performed by a life-size white marble statue of him at the ashram in 2006. Its, or rather his, mouth opened, and the lingam fell into my hands.

The entire cosmic principles of the creation, operation, and cessation of life are contained within a lingam by holding the consciousness of the whole cycle as one. Lingams are birthed to reawaken that consciousness and to give the energy of the source of that oneness, the Holy Womb and the Holy Heart that gives birth to all creation. Only the full force of this birth-life-death giving energy can heal the darkness and unconsciousness of separation by reclaiming it.

What is birthed is the inner intelligence and experience of creation as one, beyond all separate forms, the knowing and experience of what is beyond birth, beyond death, and beyond life. It is a form of the formless, energised by the supreme light of selfless wholeness.

Lingams reawaken us to our true reality by taking back aspects of our unconsciousness, energetically rebalancing us through the transmission of higher vibrations, and aligning us to our deepest and highest nature.

They come in between us and the channels of unconsciousness that threaten harm, they protect and take negativity, keep the peace, are active and dynamic peacekeepers, and prevent the total destruction and collapse of the energetic system of creation.

They hold the merging of energy and consciousness and are presented to reveal the truth behind the dualities of light and dark, masculine and feminine, life and death, me and you. They reconnect us to the cosmic mind, heart and order, and heal ego-driven unconsciousness that holds on to fear, division, violence, hate and suffering.

We receive from them the cosmic mother's womb energy for the recreation of our existence.

This form and identity of me in time and space is not the true reality of what I am. There is a power beyond of which I am, and this power alone can set me free. Creation itself has given the formulas, through the lineage of saints, so that we all can receive this freedom, manifest this freedom, and know that we are that which is beyond all form.

The second birth of a lingam that I witnessed was by Sri Kaleshwar who had already performed this delivery a number of times, generally at the annual time of Shivaratri, the night when consciousness awakens to pass on the channels of creation. This birthing happened at Shivaratri in 2008.

The students at the ashram were receiving the energy from a large supernatural lingam that had been passed from saint to saint and had been in Buddha's as well as Jesus' hands, both working with the creation channels to balance the negativity and poisons on the planet. In the middle of this process, I noticed Swami drinking in the Indian style with his head tipped back, pouring water into his mouth from a bottle without the bottle touching his lips. He wasn't swallowing.

He straightened his head and with a split-second flicker of his eyes signalled to a spot. It told me to put my hands there. As I stretched out my arms, he directed his aim and released the water from his mouth and in the outpouring came a lingam, straight into my hands.

I have used both lingams for healing ever since, as divine energy is being transmitted through each constantly

Soul Splitting

I had already been married and divorced many years before and I was not looking for a partner at the ashram, a relationship was the last distraction I wanted in my mind. However, there was someone with whom I felt a deeper connection, I will refer to him as RC. Halfway through the university year, Swami asked me if my heart was open to him. Shortly before this, Swami performed a classic supernatural manoeuvre of shooting an arrow to hit the desire energy chakra in RC and opened his eyes to me, in a fraction of a second.

Cupid's arrow in western terminology, or a Krishna arrow in eastern, to bring up the energy of attraction, of kama, that irresistible force that pulls people towards each other, and it worked. Something happened in that split second as RC took a double take at me. We were hooked. Swami asked me if I would marry him. He then planned and arranged the wedding, including the day we would get married, which we did not know until the very morning. It turned out to be on the day of Guru Purnima, the Guru's full moon when he can give the highest blessings. The ashram was full of people and Swami had a stage built. He waited for the exact time that it would rain before calling us for the ceremony and we were rained on with a torrent which is considered a huge blessing. Though RC and I had many personal differences, our faith in following our Guru's direction was strong. Many people were happy for us, they felt a sense of hope that a spiritual marriage was possible.

It was a very public marriage and brought with it many public expectations.

RC was from the USA, and I was still living in England and at the end of the University year we went to Swami to ask where we should work and live. I was unprepared when he told us to start in the USA, to give the teachings and healings. He looked at me and I looked at him as he said, "You think your life is over, don't you?" My head dropped into my hands and then he looked straight into my eyes and said three times, "I'll take care, I'll take care, I'll take care". That was the start of coming back into the world to find home and connection in a different way.

Within a month, I was heading for Los Angeles, to start a new life with a new husband. I had a huge culture shock and experienced the familiar feelings of depression that it brings. I did not recognise it until some time later, speaking with a friend who had described her own culture shock when moving to England from Serbia. I felt disconnected and displaced again.

Our marriage in India in 2007, was a spiritual one, and we would not get legally married for another four years. In the meantime, it was not possible to stay in America for longer than three months at a time as a visitor. This meant I was moving between America and England every three months, and in America we moved from place to place. We were regularly not physically together in the same place at the same time. Which as challenging as it was, it was also a blessing to not become too attached. We had married for spiritual reasons, to break the norms and the identities that come with them. And as always, this breaking has to come from within. The stage was being set and about three years later the breakup would be triggered.

In 2010, I was on the island of Saint Thomas in the US Virgin Islands at the start of a three-state tour of giving workshops for women, exploring the spiritual nature of women's energy. RC was on a three-month course at the ashram in India. I was staying on a small yacht moored in the harbour, preparing for an introductory talk that I was going to be giving that evening at a local café entitled, Women, Weight and Worry.

Early that morning my phone kept ringing, but my cell phone had poor reception and the call from RC kept dropping. He managed to call the organiser of my tour who was also a close associate and asked her to come over to me with her phone which she did hurriedly so that I could receive his call.

RC was on the other end, and I went into the cabin below to speak. With a lot of distress in his voice he told me that Swami, who had married us so publicly, was now telling him to marry someone else that very evening at the ashram and was again doing it very publicly for all to witness. We had both subscribed to surrender to the guru, to a higher power acting through the guru, and now it was being put to the test. RC was facing a dilemma. He did not want to marry someone else, and I did not want him to either.

But there was no question in my mind that this new instruction had to be followed, it was the instruction of our guru who had demonstrated he was a living embodiment of a higher power. No matter how this manifested, it was a power that was beyond any one of us, which I trusted. My response to RC was that he had to agree. I had complete trust that there was a higher reason beyond our personal feelings for each other. And we could not know that reason now, just the price we seemed to have to pay. So many times, Swami reminded us "you don't know what you're going to receive" and we cannot know until it is received.

Creation does not work to punish, only to release, it does not work to reject only to accept back.

He had blessed us to break us, to release us from our fears, if we trusted.

Our conversation ended when our phone connection died. I went back up on deck and sat.

My system slipped into an involuntary state of grief. Life had changed in a split second, and it was disorientating and overwhelming. Thoughts passed through my mind of what I would not be doing anymore, what favourite dishes I would no longer be cooking for RC, and other small and familiar things. There was a sense of loss and separation, and lots of tears. This lasted for two hours then it felt as if everything stopped and had become unusually quiet and still.

No words can adequately describe what happened next. It felt like an energetic explosion of my very being, that I had divided into infinite pieces and these infinite pieces had connected to every part of the universe. My soul had split. I was not disconnected from one human being but connected completely to every part of creation. It brought a complete and ultimate connection. How could there be any loss? There was only freedom, bliss, and unequivocal truth of there being no other to be separated from. I am everywhere, of everything. I am connected to every form, there is nothing that is not me, I belong everywhere, everything is a part of me. This was creation's blessing, experiencing the non-duality of the heart. It was an infinite fission of my core, blowing my heart to infinity.

I spoke that night at the meeting with the women, describing the short-lived human pain I experienced and how it had been turned into liberation beyond measure. I still had the same feelings for RC, even if our physical lives may have seemed to change. Most of the women related to the pain, and it brought up in them feelings of loss, anger, and betrayal. But it was for their release, and the energy continued to release, because they all received the outpouring of the blessing of freedom. They received the universal connection, the true power and nature of women's spiritual energy, and the energetic experience of the vibration of creation as a whole and undivided creation.

Several hours later, RC called again and said that Swami had called the whole thing off, but something had broken between us. Even though we stayed together, we were not going to recover enough to enjoy the flight our souls could take together in freedom.

Public expectations were shattered too and in that, some hearts also found their freedom.

Swami taught that the soul, the energy of life, enters the body through the spiritual heart, and he demonstrated that the soul could leave the body through the heart. An open heart is like a diamond, knowing and reflecting all as itself, without conflict, without opposition, without struggle, without separation. It is everything, unconditionally. It is what a mother feels for a child, what creation feels for every part of itself, there is no attachment to one and not another. He also taught that heartbreak is one of the major causes of pain and suffering in the world, an irreconcilable longing to be free from the confinement of perceived separation. Women are particularly susceptible to this, but once resolved, are especially well placed to implement the energy of wholeheartedness, the energy of the womb. No partial or temporary attachment can ever truly fulfill the heart, only the universal attachment to creation, and for that the heart must leave the confines of the body and know its connection to everything.

Now I had experienced the most profound union with the universal heart; an unconditional and infinite belonging, with the universal mind; an awareness of all as self, and with the universal soul; the ultimate source of all power. I could start to implement the healing channels of this union energy for the freedom of others.

Swami left his body about eighteen months later in 2012. He had given the transmission of the supernatural reality and the formulas for the transmission; mantras that directly awaken the highest vibrations. He wanted to leave this legacy so that as many souls as possible could receive the tools to come out of unnecessary suffering and awaken to their authentic and divinely given birthright, the right to know the oneness of creation as self. Before leaving, he embodied this birthright, the energy of the womb that gives birth to all of creation, in a large murti at the ashram, a statue embodying the divine energy, for all who come in front of her to receive.

The form of creation embodying the healing of separation, is that of Kanakadurga.

The Angel of Liberation

Over the next five years, I practiced with the free energy of heart, mind, and soul. Going in and out of myself and connecting this freedom to objects, and to people for healing, to awaken the vibration of inseparable connection and release the pain inherent in the unknowing of this eternal connection

On one occasion during this time, I was again on the island of Saint Thomas, giving a class on healing. I had used a particular venue many times for talks, classes and spiritual processes, which had created a vibration in the space that stayed and was readily available to connect with. For some time, a small group had been looking at the nature of violence, corruption, and disintegration of society, and had the intention to build a spiritual army, an army of angelic liberators.

They were a specially gathered group of women who understood the feminine nature, the nature of connection to universal power through the womb and an undivided heart and mind.

The intention was to work with the angels who were the channels of that power, the active and dynamic power of universal love and healing, of truth, justice and peace. We would create an army strong enough to defeat the strongest forms of negativity and reclaim the unconsciousness. The energy of the womb of creation itself, unbound by ego, able to change any part of itself, of which there is nothing stronger.

After a little while in meditation using certain mantra formulas, a deep peace descended upon the roomful of women, along with an upsurge of energy. Each woman had a different experience during and after the meditation. Some saw statues come alive and move, some saw a presence appear in a particular form they were familiar with, some felt a vibration around them, and some heard messages. To me, the power presenting was the embodiment of the freedom of creation, the channel of the freedom of creation, and the fulfilment of our intentions. It was an intimate knowing experience, a presentation of the Angel of Liberation, the remover of illusions, the remover of darkness and deliverer into freedom. It was Kanakadurga, the power of freedom, connecting to each person present. I was immediately aware that it was the same energy that Martin Luther King had connected to, that Gandhi had connected to, and that Moses had connected to.

The same energy that Jesus, Buddha, Mohammed and all the great liberators of the ages had connected to.

It was the power of liberation itself, the healing power of creation, the power to heal destruction, and the power of protection and preservation of the laws of creation. It was an energy that could connect anywhere, be sent to anyone, to open the pathways of freedom from the stranglehold of duality and fear. It could change what was in someone's heart and mind and give the energy for a different outcome. Just as I had witnessed the parting of the sea of illusions before my own eyes, I witnessed this power as its source. When Nelson Mandela died, I felt this same energy released from his soul, and knew that he too had connected to it. This freed-from-the body energy, when left behind, becomes even more accessible to be received by others, it is an energetic legacy that most great souls leave.

I practised for a further three years to connect this channel of freedom to systems of healing in water; the medium of the womb energy, in meditation circles, and to places. Always for the purpose of transmitting and passing on the healing vibrations.

Swami's mission was to mend the broken bridge between humanity and the reality of creation. He gave the formulas for this reunification, for the awakening of the channel of freedom. This power, Kanakadurga, roughly translates as 'the invincible light that defeats the demons of ignorance'. Swami manifested this power on earth and gave us the means to connect to her, the divine and ultimate power of the feminine, the mother and master healer of all. Bringing her power of freedom to life defeats the ignorance of duality that is the ego which divides and oppresses.

Challenge for the Channels

Only five months before Swami left his body, taking his ultimate samadhi, RC and I were finally legally married. We had been through a tough year after RC's cancelled second marriage, but I did not doubt that we could move ahead together, and we actively planned my move to the US. But as the last days of Swami's physical life were unfolding, so too, our marriage was dying.

When a saint leaves his body there is always the passing on of energy that had been initiated and purposefully planned beforehand, as well as chaos, fragmentation and disharmony, as claims to his/her legacy are made from the rising of egos. A saint's energy, consciousness, and channels to creation are passed on in many different ways; particularly Swami's, whose mission it was to enable the channels of pure vibration to unfold in as many people as possible and for each person to flower in that vibration with their own fragrance. Each student that Swami taught was a branch of the mission, a fragrance in the divine garden to be passed on, each an expression of miracle energy that was part of the same soil, supporting the growth of each. There can be no exclusivity in true spirituality, just as there cannot be in humanity, but as the spiritual metaphor for unconsciousness is the wave believing it is separate to other waves or even a separate ocean, so too spiritual students seemed to display a belief that their branch was the true and only tree. And this also manifested within my marriage.

No spiritual adherent looks, acts, speaks, or practises exactly like another or can even understand the other's practise or manner.

We are not shaped in a mould, rather it is our own moulds that we strive to break, each releasing a channel for that breaking.

During those last months and days of Swami's physical life, I felt like I was being killed, that I was being sucked dry of life, and not just because it was the hottest and driest time of the year before the rains, with temperatures around 100 degrees fahrenheit. What was being killed in that intense transmission right up to the end? We were all receiving the channels of creation which kill negativity. It is a spiritual truth that we have to experience suffering to know the remedy to that suffering, that the remedy can only be revealed in the suffering, to truly know how that suffering is transformed. I was being killed to know that I can rise in a different relationship with creation and receive the means by which others can be brought out of negativity. We all were receiving the gift which overcomes even as we feel overcome.

I had to go through the playing out of being hung out to dry in my marriage. It was the final gift. So after Swami's samadhi and cutting my physical ties in England, the paperwork for me to remain in the US, which I was dependent upon RC to submit, was not completed. It felt like a betrayal. I started the next five years of my life living out of two suitcases and moving constantly, sometimes after a few days and sometimes after a few weeks, and this time there was no home to go back to. Many times, I did not know where I was going to sleep the next night or the next week.

The question still remained, where was my home?

But I had learnt from earlier years the value of being present and grateful in the moment, of taking one day at a time, one night at a time. I knew I had to carry on giving the teachings and healings as Swami had directed and my trust and faith was more powerful than any discomfort or challenge. In fact, it only served to strengthen my trust and faith, as the more challenged I was, the more trusting a faith I had, no matter what it looked like.

Trust, faith, and practise in something greater than your own experience brings rewards, it brings the fruit of that trust to life.

Power of the Womb

At the end of another retreat on Saint Thomas in 2014, I was asked to hold an extra class on the teachings of the Holy Womb Chakra. This new, yet ancient teaching, had been given by Swami in the process of revealing the channels to the divine mother of creation herself. It is her profound energy system that births, sustains and takes back all forms of creation. It is the mechanism of the whole cycle of birth, life, and death and more importantly, what gives rise to it, the origin of nature as a whole.

The knowledge of this energy system is given so that we can understand our nature, our true origin in creation's wholeness, and be healed of our own misunderstandings, misinterpretations and false beliefs of who we think we are, separated and divided. It puts us back in direct and right relationship with creation and everything that is creation. In short, it sets us free from all forms that entrap us in an identity, and allows us to know our eternal formless nature regardless of the form we may take in this life, the last, or the next. It takes us out of our belief in, and attachment to, any form for our survival, we can let go of fear and know that we are the completeness of what is beyond.

We are non-dependent and non-determined by form, or by identity of any kind.

This unconditional power of the Holy Womb of creation came to life and revealed itself within me.

We had just finished several days of meditation, mainly taking place in a private pool of water, and people were making their way off the island and back to their respective homes. Some, however, were staying behind and had asked for some additional meditation and instruction. The topic they requested was the Holy Womb Chakra. As usual, I spent time in preparation and meditation but there was something different about this meditation.

We were still in the full moon energy, and I am always aware at these times of being pulled strongly inwards, deep beyond myself, yet this pull seemed stronger than normal. I could feel its power, and it was as if it were not sucking me in, but rather sucking out everything around me. I was awake and conscious but there was no body, I was sitting on the floor yet there was no floor, the room with its chairs and pictures in which we had spent so many hours meditating no longer existed.

It was the most peaceful, powerful, blissful feeling I

had ever experienced, being complete with nothing. There was no time in this infinite space, yet outwardly time must have passed as I was later told that the participants for the class had been waiting for some time outside the door to our classroom. They had been waiting to be let in as the door had become mysteriously locked. The energy had not allowed them to enter until it was time and had alerted me to their knocking. I was in my body, but I was not it, my mind was functioning, but I was not it. As the group sat down to listen, it became clear that it was not a teaching they were there for, but a transmission of energy and they had to be open enough to receive it.

Being open means not holding on to what is in your own mind, your ideas and your intentions, what you want to do or what you do not want to do, but to be willing to be moved, to be taken beyond those very limitations.

A couple of people were late, preoccupied with what they were thinking they had to do at that time, and only just made it in before the door was locked again. I could barely keep my eyes open, yet I looked at each one in turn knowing that they were receiving an initiation of the Holy Womb energy, the very power of creation itself, tangible and real.

The looks in their eyes varied, revealing what they were there to let go of, to be relieved of, to be healed of. For some it was doubt, for some fear, for some longing, for some loss, and for others, old stories of pain. I could speak but I could barely get the words out, yet I was still able to address each in turn with a message or an instruction or a mantra particular to each.

Most did not realise what was happening at the time, what was manifesting in front of them and for them.

It can take some time for the energy to be digested and integrated back through the mind-body system; energy always comes first, and then the understanding of it comes later.

As awakened kundalini is the energy and consciousness of the soul freed from the restrictions of the body, the Holy Womb Chakra is the centre in the body through which that energy and consciousness manifests. It can transport us to the very beginning of time, to the heart and soul of creation. There is no power greater than that of the Holy Womb, it is invincible and is known in Sanskrit as Durga, the primordial cosmic energy of which there is nothing beyond. The Holy Womb Chakra is connected to the physical womb of women, and it is therefore women who have the most immediate, sacred and profound access to this immeasurable and irreducible power.

Women hold the power of freedom, the freedom that is the unified energy of the womb which reclaims all egos.

Durga, the ultimate controller of power and form of shakti, and therefore controller of ignorance of that power which includes pride, was manifesting and being transmitted. Power was present, flowing through me, speaking through me, acting through me, and at my feet was the pulsating subtle energy body of a tiger, Durga's vehicle, calm and controlled. The infinite power of the womb of creation was manifesting herself through my body to transmit healing.

This presentation in our classroom by our energised pool of water lasted for about twenty minutes and then I gradually came back into a 'normal' state of mind and body feeling. For the next twenty-four hours it was as if I was suffering from a hangover, an energy hangover though with a high energy feeling still running as well as the heaviness of an overload.

Over the next few years, my system gradually became accustomed to the all-encompassing power and presence without the hangover. Physically, I returned to Eastbourne, but what I had been shown, beyond a shadow of a doubt, was that home was truly within me. Home, complete connection and belonging, where I am wanted, is within the creation that is within me.

The power of unity to end division is within me and there can be no displacement from that.

This Holy Womb energy is a unified field of energy and consciousness as a whole, which informs every part and particle, and transmits itself to restore humanity. If we seek a unified world, we must recognise and awaken this unified indivisible power, the pure power that is within each one of us and more directly linked to women. If we seek a divided world from which many think they have much to gain because of their own internal separation and displacement, then women and the element closely linked with womb energy - water - will be controlled, abused, and polluted. But a self-righting system cannot be disturbed forever. Durga will rise, the energy of belonging to bring us all back to our true soul home that we share as one.

This energy has been embodied in Kanakadurga Peace Statues around the world, bringing home all who come in front of her.

Our Shared Story

I had a relatively short spiritual training, but those six years under Swami's personal guidance were intense. He delivered the techniques that he said he would and answered everything that I sought.

He gave the teachings, and their precise methods of transmission, of Mother Mary, Jesus, Buddha, and of many other Saints so that we could have the true mechanisms of love and power to heal suffering and liberate our potential.

His training brought down the walls between the natural and supernatural, for our freedom to be experienced whilst we are in form, a new form of experience.

The formulas are our short-cuts to activating our freedom, awakening our soul vibration, and discovering the creation that we are.

This is a personal and collective journey of healing, from trauma and displacement, disconnection and division to universal freedom and connection. It takes us to a power and presence beyond anything imaginable. We have been given the formulas to know that we belong beyond any and every definition, to end conflicts of identification that perpetuate fear of not belonging and the illusion of separation. To merge with the power and consciousness of creation itself and to voyage on the wings of angels.

It is the story of my family, of anyone marginalised or disenfranchised, just as it is the story of those perpetrating disharmony and conflict. It is a shared story of unconscious belief in separation and the fear that drives and holds it, whichever portrayal of the story we enact. Yet, our story can change to one where we can experience the true power of love, protecting, connecting, and freeing; conquering fear which attacks, divides, and suffocates, whether inflicted upon ourselves or others. The power of liberation is in everyone's hands, their hearts and souls, waiting to be awakened.

Something of my Indian spiritual heritage, and the power of Penukonda, had been stored in my family's memory. A knowledge and belief in this liberating power had been retained through the generations, however distant and inert.

That soul sense of belonging to a supernatural force that brings us home, though out of sight for so long, was ready to be reawakened and brought to life. I am indebted to my ancestors for enduring their journey of displacement, and to all those who still do and are looking for their freedom, compelling me to seek the remedies to the pain of separation that can endure for generations. To seek out and to be granted the formulas of freedom, for freedom to take form. To know that there is no separation.

When our soul, mind and heart have no walls, no artificial walls of thoughts, beliefs or actions can ever be real or hold power over us.

This story is for all who search for freedom.

Peace Circles

Swami gave precise mantra formulas to connect to the divine power of the mother of creation, to her womb energy, shakti. To bring her active and dynamic healing through each soul to dispel fear and darkness, and for the true seat of power to be recognised within each and within the world. She is what is beyond but also what is most immanent when her vibrations are awakened. It is her womb energy that both men and women can connect to, though women more quickly and adeptly.

Some of these formulas are used in the meditation system of Peace Circles; a healing practice to overcome personal and global stress and conflict. These meditation circles are open to anyone, with or without any prior spiritual experience, and are applicable to bringing down all types of barriers and conflict. Peace Circles are led by trained facilitators.

I teach and train only from direct experience, and the

formulation of the Peace Circles method is the direct result of my life's spiritual process and purpose to pass on the divine channels of freedom, the channels of the mother of my life that is the mother of your life. Trained Peace Circles Initiators around the world hold Peace Circles to continue the flow of her divine life force, the vibration of unconditional cosmic connection. Many more are needed to become the active instruments to implement the love and power that is the energy of our birthright and our homecoming.

If you wish to connect with Peace Circles near you, or to become a Peace Circles Initiator, please visit my website healing4humanity.com/peace-circles

Shakti, the Universal Mother of Creation is the existential energy of freedom that overcomes our deepest fears of separation and extinction, leading us to awaken to a new world and a new life.

Jai Ma!

About Nadira

Nadira Seeram was born in Guyana of Indian heritage to her parents Karamchand and Savitri and raised in England.

Living with a legacy of displacement and societies' separatisms her life's journey has been to rediscover the heart of connection in humanity.

Trained in western psychotherapy she sought answers to deeper existential questions and found them in her eastern spiritual heritage.

Experiencing supernatural phenomena and practising ancient formulas revealed not only how to bring the soul out of the mind-body system but out of any fear-based system.

Bringing together an intimate knowledge of both mind-body and soul-consciousness systems, she has worked since 2007 as a spiritual therapist, teacher, and trainer of meditation facilitators to reclaim the forgotten freedom for the planet.

Nadira recognises the heart of humanity as the universal constant to which all belong, and the lineages of informed souls who hold the way open for this discovery including her revered Guru Sri Kaleshwar.

In honour of the one divine power beyond all duality, "She is what I am".

h4h
Completing the Way

Healing 4 Humanity

The work of Healing 4 Humanity is the work of changing our individual and collective story, dedicated to bringing out the supernatural spirit of connection in our natural world.

There is a true wholeness behind any act of division, we can reclaim it, bring it to life and make it our reality.

Contact Nadira to find out about more, by visiting healing4humanity.com

For information on Indentureship visit The Ameena Gafoor Institute: ameenagafoorinstitute.org

For further information on Sri Kaleshwar visit Sri Kaleshwar World: srikaleshwar.world and the Journeys With Kaleshwar Archive: journeyswithkaleshwar.org

Sri Kaleshwar® is a registered trademark of Shirdi Sai Global Trust, Shiva Sai Mandir Penukonda, Anantapur District 515110, India.

Lightning Source UK Ltd.
Milton Keynes UK
UKHW010519220822
407537UK00002B/50

'It Is Beyond Me' is a book of immense hope. It charts the path of a family crossing continents, it is a story of dispossession, physical, mental and emotional distress but with the thread of intrinsic connection that is followed all the way back to its beginning.

These are first-hand accounts of rare supernatural phenomena described with meaning and purpose. We see the work of a living avatar channelling supernatural mechanisms of healing and teaching the formulas for liberation.

Above all, it acclaims the bringing to life of the divine feminine force with the ultimate power to dismantle fear and reconnect humanity. This book is a homecoming, not only to the land of family origin but to the formulas of the origin of all. Having found the answers, the author hopes this book will touch and inspire many to continue their own journey to freedom, and to become spiritually armed to help bring freedom to so many in need.

The cover photo is the Dove of Peace (spiritual eye) that appeared on a cloth after it held a lingam being used for healing.

h4h
Completing the Way
healing4humanity.com

Non Fiction   UK £6.99

ISBN 978-1-7397579-0-8

9 781739 757908

90000